SHABBAT

CELEBRATING THE SABBATH
THE MESSIANIC JEWISH WAY

Richard & Michele
Berkowitz

LEDERER PUBLICATIONS
BALTIMORE, MARYLAND

We lovingly dedicate this work to our children

Beth
Rachel
Rebekah
Joel

May they love Shabbat, and love him
who is the Lord of the Sabbath,
Yeshua who loved us and caused us
to enter into the eternal rest found only in him.

Unless otherwise noted, verses from *Tenakh,* the "Older" Testament are from *The Holy Bible,* New International Version ©1978 and 1983 by New York International Bible Society. New Covenant scriptures are from the *Jewish New Testament* by Dr. David Stern ©1989 Jewish New Testament Publications, Jerusalem, Israel and Clarksville, Md., used by permission.

Third printing with revisions.

Cover by Devorah Goldberg.
Other illustrations by Steffi Rubin and Devorah Goldberg.
Copyright ©1988 and 1991 by Richard and Michele Berkowitz
ISBN 1-880226-00-6
Printed in the United States of America

TABLE OF CONTENTS

INTRODUCTION

Rest!

What a blissful word. The very mention of it suggests hours of reclining in a favorite easy chair, munching a bagel and sipping tea or coffee in front of a warm cozy fire.

But pleasurable as rest is, few people enjoy the blessing of it. Perhaps there is not time for it. Perhaps "rest" sounds synonymous with "laziness." Perhaps some simply don't know how to enjoy it. It is a tragic fact that in our fast-paced world many simply don't schedule rest into their appointment books.

This book discusses rest and God's purpose for it. God is vitally interested in helping us understand the whole concept of rest as *he* defines it. And, because God is for rest, we should be for it, too.

In this brief, practical guide you will understand not only the meaning of God's rest day—*Shabbat* (pronounced Sha-**baht**) or Sabbath—but also ways to make it an important part of your week. While this is not intended to be a theological treatise on the Sabbath, it is necessary to lay a solid theological foundation upon which to build an observance of this day. Therefore, the first section of this guide will describe the purpose of celebrating Shabbat. The second section will focus on methods of observing it. And the third section will be our challenge to you.

With this in mind, relax on your recliner, a bagel in one hand, your Bible in your lap and this guide in the other hand. Begin to learn how to make Shabbat a delight for your family. CAUTION! This tradition could become habit-forming!

PART I

WHY SHOULD MESSIANIC JEWS (AND GENTILES) OBSERVE SHABBAT?

Any celebration of Shabbat done with the hope of *earning points* with God should not be done at all. As Messianic Jews and Gentile believers, we trust the Scriptures which state:

> *...he delivered us....not on the ground of any righteous deeds we had done, but on the ground of his own mercy. He did it by means of the* mikveh [baptism] *of rebirth and the renewal brought about by the* Ruach HaKodesh [Holy Spirit], *whom he poured out on us generously through* Yeshua [Jesus] *the Messiah, our Deliverer* (Titus 3:5–6).

From this we learn that we should not observe Shabbat in order to earn or add to the completed atoning work of Messiah on our behalf. That being true, then why should Messianic people observe Shabbat?

A COVENANT SIGN

One reason for the observance of Shabbat is given in Exodus 31:12–17. God tells Israel to observe Shabbat, the seventh day rest period, as a *sign* of his promises to her. The Hebrew word for sign indicates a pledge or a token of what is promised. God made certain promises to Israel, and gave the Shabbat as a visible token of his commitment to keep those promises.

In ancient times, when a king entered into a covenant with a lesser nation, he would have his own sign engraved in the middle of the agreement. This was done to guarantee that he would keep his part of the covenant. Quite often the sign would assume the form of the king's god or gods.

Likewise, the terms of God's covenant with his vassal nation Israel are here in Exodus. He had already made some of these agreements with Abraham years before. Now, in the midst of this legal covenant document, God gives a sign that will serve to remind the nation that he intends to remain their God and has called them for specific reasons. Rather than an image of himself, God chose the seventh day— the day of rest and worship—as the sign of this covenant. This serves as a unique testimony to the special relationship between God and Israel.

The Shabbat sign is like a big banner held up once a week inscribed with the words, "Israel has been set apart by God. It is God's doing; he intends to keep his promises to Israel." Let's let the banners fly and remind ourselves of God's promises to his people.

A PERFECT PICTURE

The New Covenant clearly shows that God intended to use many of the ceremonial practices in the Torah as pictures of the spiritual realities we have in Yeshua. Included in these practices are the feasts of Israel. The letter to *Messianic Jews (Hebrews)* specifically mentions *Yom Kippur* (the Day of Atonement) and Shabbat. We will not comment here on *Yom Kippur*, but let's see what we can learn from Shabbat.

So there remains a Shabbat-keeping for God's people. For the one who has entered God's rest has also rested from his own works, as God did from his. Therefore, let us do our best to enter that rest, so that no one will fall short because of the same kind of disobedience (Messianic Jews 4:9–11).

And Yeshua taught, "Shabbat was made for mankind, not mankind for Shabbat; so the Son of Man is Lord even of Shabbat" (Mark 2:27).

These portions show us that the Sabbath was given by God to provide a key to understanding how to enter into the full riches of one of his spectacular mysteries: Messiah, in whom are hidden all the treasures of wisdom and knowledge. To unravel this mystery and see the role Shabbat has, let's begin at the very beginning.

By the seventh day God had finished the work he had been doing; so on the seventh day he rested from all his work. And God blessed the seventh day and made it holy, because on it he rested from all the work of creating that he had done (Genesis 2:2–3).

When God, in eternity past, planned the creation of the world, he chose to do so in a way that would emphasize the centrality of the seventh day rest. Here we see that rest following six days of labor.

Later, God emphasized the seventh day rest as part of the covenant he made with Israel. In his teaching on the Shabbat, God emphasized the cessation of all work, saying,

Six days you shall labor and do all your work, but the seventh day is a Sabbath to the Lord your God. On it you shall not do any work, neither you, nor your son or daughter, nor your manservant or maidservant...nor the alien within your gates, so that your manservant and maidservant may rest, as you do (Deuteronomy 5:13–14).

The emphasis was on *rest*. Why? The picture begins to unfold in the next verse. Deuteronomy 5:15 states,

Remember that you were slaves in Egypt and that the Lord your God brought you out of there with a mighty hand and an outstretched arm. Therefore the Lord your God has commanded you to observe the Sabbath day.

God says specifically that the Sabbath day of rest was to be, among other things, a weekly reminder to Israel of his miraculous and momentous deliverance from slavery in Egypt to rest as a free nation.

Just as God took Israel down into Egypt and allowed them to be slaves to Pharaoh who worked them without rest, believers too were slaves in Satan's kingdom under the bondage of sin (Romans 6:17). Moreover, just as Israel could not deliver herself out of physical bondage, no one is able to deliver himself out of bondage to sin. The reasons are found in the Scripture—we were dead spiritually in our own sins and therefore lacked any ability of our own (Roman 3:10–12; Ephesians 2:1).

Just as it took the mighty hand of God and his outstretched arm to deliver Israel from slavery and to inflict judgment on Egypt, so too it took a great miracle and display of God's judgment on sin and Satan to deliver his chosen ones. This deliverance was accomplished when Yeshua atoned for sin, thereby setting men free and inflicting judgment on Satan's kingdom (Ephesians 1:7; 1:13–14; 2:13–15).

In other words, the believer's life before rebirth is six days of slave labor. Then *Shabbat* which is Messiah Yeshua. *He* is the end of the "six days" for it is through him that one enters the "seventh day rest." God requires that his people stop working for righteousness, and rest in the finished work of Messiah.

Shabbat, therefore, becomes a key to understanding life in Messiah. It is a Sabbath rest—an eternal Sabbath rest! Believers have ceased from all labor, striving to please God, and have rested in him. It is complete. No longer in the "six days" of slavery to sin, believers are free men and women, born of God, and heirs of his kingdom. Now, through faith in Messiah, one enters the Sabbath rest of God. "For the one who has entered God's rest has also rested from his own works, as God did from his" (Messianic Jews 4:9).

Shabbat is the perfect picture. God painted it to help his people understand what life in Messiah is to be. That picture and an awareness of the covenant sign of Shabbat, help us see why Messianic Jews and Gentiles should celebrate Shabbat. But there is more.

A WEEKLY OBSERVANCE

It is easy to understand the glorious picture of Shabbat which God painted for us. But why is it necessary to see that picture every week? We believe God's reason is intimately connected with the picture of his rest, the Shabbat.

Our flesh pulls us to return to a life of "doing" to achieve righteousness. Remember how Israel wanted to return to Egypt? So does our flesh. We must therefore make "every effort" to *remain* in our Sabbath rest spiritually. As it is written in Galatians 5:1, "What the Messiah freed us for is freedom!" It is essential that we remember not to try to establish our own righteousness. Let it never be said of us,

> *You stupid [believers]! Who has put you under a spell? Before your very eyes Yeshua the Messiah was clearly portrayed as having been put to death as a criminal! I want to know from you just this one thing: did you receive the Spirit by legalistic observance of Torah commands or by trusting in what you heard and being faithful to it? Are you that stupid? Having begun with the Spirit's power, do you think you can reach the goal under your own power?* (Galatians 3:1–3)

Our new life in Messiah is a faith walk, not a works walk. It is ceasing moment-by-moment from "self-effort" and remaining in the Sabbath rest which we entered through Yeshua. Unfortunately, we are so forgetful! But, our all-knowing God has provided for this shortcoming! After every six days, we have a remembrance —a physical Sabbath day—to remind us anew of our spiritual freedom in him.

In the Tenach, there are at least two passages which teach that we are to observe Shabbat "so that you may know" something (Exodus 31:12–13 and Ezekiel 20:12) to be reminded of certain truths about us, God's elect. Specifically, the passages teach us that God wants Shabbat to remind us of who we are as redeemed people. He wants us to know he has set us apart and made us holy unto him. He wants to remind us that we are his prized possession. In other words, in light of New Covenant truth, God wants to reassure us that we are no longer slaves, but free, newly created people, born anew from God in Messiah Yeshua.

Hence, a major purpose for the weekly celebration of Shabbat is so that God can lovingly remind us of who we are in him.

Let us therefore learn to "remain." Understanding and observing the Shabbat will help us learn to remain. Can you now see why we should remember the Shabbat in a very specific way, once a week? This day tells us that the Sabbath rest into which we have entered through faith in Messiah is an on-going rest! He has provided a weekly reminder—the Shabbat. This weekly observance paints a sacred picture of what it is like to be united in faith with Messiah Yeshua.

A BLESSING FROM ABOVE

One other reason to observe Shabbat is *God has a blessing for us*.

Isaiah 58:13–14 records God's promise of blessing for Israel's proper Shabbat observance:

> *If you keep your feet from breaking the Sabbath and from doing as you please on my holy day, if you call the Sabbath a delight and the Lord's holy day honorable, and if you honor it by not going your own way and not doing as you please or speaking idle words, then you will find your joy in the Lord, and I will cause you to ride on the heights of the land and to feast on the inheritance of your father Jacob. The mouth of the Lord has spoken.*

If we observe Shabbat in its intended way, we will experience the joy of the Lord in a unique and fresh way. Why? Because in observing Shabbat, we serve the Lord, our minds and hearts on him, the Lord of Shabbat. Also, our bodies receive their needed rest en-abling us to be fresh in our weekday service of him.

Furthermore, Isaiah told Judah that those who live in *Eretz Yisrael* (the land of Israel) would experience high productivity from their land. Could we not also say that for all of us, God promises to bless our efforts if we observe Shabbat? There is a catch, however.

We must take God at his word; *that* is true faith. God's secret to *finding* the joy in the Lord that is ours in Messiah is having the right attitude: to delight in the Lord and not do what our flesh desires. If we keep Shabbat the way God designed it, he himself will cause us to *ride* on the heights of the land and *feast* on the inheritance of our father Jacob. It is a promise! Simple, but eternally profound!

It is not enough just to set aside the seventh day and do as *we* want. The blessings God has in store for us are commensurate with *how* we observe Shabbat. The methods of observing Shabbat which are given in the next section of this book will help you have the right focus for your Shabbat.

PART II

HOW MESSIANIC JEWS
(AND GENTILES)
CAN OBSERVE SHABBAT

SHABBAT PREPARATION

It was Preparation Day,
and a Shabbat was about to begin (Luke 23:54).

Such an important day, set apart for blessing, requires special preparation. This preparation begins with prayer. The observance of God's Sabbath is so central to our victorious walk that it will most certainly come under the attack of the Evil One. In addition, we can no more carry out the will of our Father without prayer than Messiah could carry out the will of his Father without prayer.

We include here some ideas that you may want to incorporate upon waking Friday morning, the preparation day. Since the wife is usually the one at home, she may be the one to do this, although both husband and wife could do so.

■ Read Ezekiel 20:12

Also I gave them my Sabbaths as a sign between us, so they would know that I the LORD made them holy.

■ Read Messianic Jews (Hebrews) 4:9–11 (see page 9).

■ Pray:

I thank you, O God, for our salvation. I pray that you would make this coming Sabbath Day a reminder and use it as a teaching tool for us and for our children. As we enter into and stay in your Sabbath rest, grant deeper wisdom, insight and understanding this week to each one of us and to our family, including our congregation family.

Lord, give us your wisdom as to how to keep this Sabbath day holy. Thank you for giving us one day of rest each week to have undistracted time to worship you and to remember our relationship with you. Lord, may we be reminded of your provisions this Sabbath day.

■ Read Isaiah 58:13–14 (see page 12).

■ Mother prays:

Father, I come against every plan of the Evil One to destroy our Shabbat. Use me as a vessel to prepare our home and our meal as a setting for us to appreciate you.

■ Father prays:

This Sabbath home is an holy place; I want your power, Lord, to function as a holy priest to perform divine services in it.

We have gained insight from our own experience. In order to have a successful Sabbath day, we must have a successful preparation day. Keeping this in mind, we schedule all family plans and activities—including regular housework and special jobs—Sunday through Thursday so that Friday remains free. A Friday overwhelmed with too much work to finish before sundown will not allow enough time for needed Shabbat preparation. It is wonderful to wake up Friday morning knowing that enough of the household is in order, and final Shabbat preparation can begin.

Those of us who have young children would do well to prepare the children to enter into the excitement of preparation. It is necessary to instill in the children the mind-set that Friday afternoon is a time of preparation for them, too. They need to feel how wonderful it is to help set the table, get dressed for Shabbat, and be free of other thoughts or activities which take the focus off Shabbat, soon to arrive.

Preparation for Shabbat really begins at the end of the previous Shabbat and culminates on Friday. But don't stop here, there's more that needs to be done before the *Erev Shabbat* (Friday evening) meal.

1. MAKE CHALLAH—THE SABBATH BREAD
(pronounced **khal**-lah) See Appendix B

The word *challah* was first used in the *Torah* (Leviticus 24:5) to describe the twelve showbreads arranged on the altar in the Tabernacle. The two loaves of challah on the Shabbat table represent the two rows of showbread displayed in the Tabernacle and Temple.

The more traditional explanation, however, is that there are two *challot* because while the children of Israel wandered in the wilderness, God miraculously fed them with *manna*, bread from heaven. On the sixth day so much *manna* fell that the people were able to collect extra portions for the Sabbath day; therefore, they were able to rest on Shabbat.

We teach our children another truth by emphasizing the double blessings God gives us when we put him first in everything we do. Furthermore, the challah on the table reminds us of Messiah Yeshua—the Bread of Life. Placing proper emphasis on Yeshua serves to focus the entire Shabbat on him who gives us rest. As you can see, the challah

15

provides an excellent opportunity to teach our children the meaning of life in Yeshua —the bread of life.

One more tidbit concerning the challah. When my wife makes challah, she prays. She prays for each of our children while kneading the dough. Her prayer is that God may give them the spirit of wisdom and revelation so that they may know him deeper. She asks God to make their hearts enlightened in order that they may know the hope to which he has called them, the riches of his glorious inheritance as believers, and the incomparable power for those who believe.

Next, she prays for one specific member or family in our congregation. After she has formed the two loaves for our family, she makes a small *baby* loaf braided like the others. At services, this baby challah will be given to the person or family for whom she prayed. The smile on their faces and the unity this gives to the congregation makes this a valuable task.

2. GET DRESSED AND PRAY

The Shabbat meal is a special occasion. In order to give it its proper honor, we make a habit of dressing up, thereby adding dignity to the occasion of welcoming the Shabbat Queen (as Shabbat is often called) in royal fashion.

After we finish getting dressed, we gather the children for prayer. We do this because the Evil One does not like a biblical Shabbat observance! He will do all he can to use children, interruptions, our flesh, or anything else to disrupt our Shabbat observance. Therefore, we pray to the Lord to protect us against the schemes of the powers of darkness and to grant us the proper spirit to bless him on the Shabbat.

3. SET THE TABLE

Before the meal begins, there are a few items that need to be in place on the dinner table. Spread your best white table cloth. Set the table with your finest dishes. Make sure wine glasses are distributed and your decanter is filled with red wine or concord grape juice. You will also need two candlesticks with white candles. (Most grocery stores supply Shabbat candles which come seventy-two in a box and burn for approximately three hours.) Finally, save a place on which to rest the challah you worked so hard to prepare. One loaf is sliced; the other is left whole. Both are placed under a special cover.

The cover can be hand made (see Appendix B) or purchased at any Jewish bookstore. (You can also buy Kiddush cups—ceremonial wine goblets—there.) Some families like to place the mama's veil, worn to symbolize submission to her husband and the papa's *kippah* or *yarmulka* (skull caps) worn to symbolize submission to God, at the place where they sit—just so they don't forget.

Now, having the table set, the children properly clothed, and your Shabbat guide ready, you are prepared for the first Shabbat event, the Friday evening *Erev Shabbat* meal.

4. SHALL WE DINE?

It is a time-honored tradition to initiate Shabbat by having a royal dinner. As Messianic believers, we think the Shabbat dinner is a worthy tradition and suggest that you too make it a very special affair. Some of us can recall how our grandparents told us about skimping throughout the week in order to set aside every penny for the Sabbath meal. When the awaited day arrived, all poverty was forgotten and a royal feast was held.

In Appendix B you will find some tasty recipes which can help to make the Friday evening meal a delectable delight. In addition to the main course, there are two items which should always be present on the Shabbat table: wine or grape juice and challah. These two items are used to help welcome Shabbat and to facilitate much of the celebration and discussion.

At this point, we will take you through a typical *Erev Shabbat* meal and explain the important symbolism and rationale for what we do. Most of the "ritual" is traditional, but some is new. Perhaps you can develop your own spiritual ingredients which will nourish your family's soul.

With this book we intend to encourage and help those of you who do not normally observe Shabbat or who may be unfamiliar with many of the Jewish Shabbat observances. To those of you wondering "Why didn't they include———?" we say, "Teach us." We have found several Shabbat home ritual guides, all of them different. Indeed, there are many traditions, prayers and blessings for Shabbat. This book is intended to help those who are just beginning family Shabbat observance. For this reason, we've kept it simple.

EREV SHABBAT—THE ORDER OF SERVICE

1. RECITATION OF V'SHAMRU

■ The first recitation is Exodus 31:16–17 which states the reason we are having this special observance. *V'Shamru* can be spoken or sung; there is a traditional chant that can be used. The words are as follows:

וְשָׁמְרוּ בְנֵי יִשְׂרָאֵל אֶת הַשַּׁבָּת,
לַעֲשׂוֹת אֶת הַשַּׁבָּת לְדֹרֹתָם בְּרִית עוֹלָם.
בֵּינִי וּבֵין בְּנֵי יִשְׂרָאֵל אוֹת הִיא לְעוֹלָם,
כִּי שֵׁשֶׁת יָמִים עָשָׂה יְיָ
אֶת הַשָּׁמַיִם וְאֶת הָאָרֶץ,
וּבַיּוֹם הַשְּׁבִיעִי שָׁבַת וַיִּנָּפַשׁ.

V'shamru b'nay Yisrael et ha-Shabbat
La-asot et ha-Shabbat l'dorotam b'rit olam.
Baynee oo-vayn b'nay Yisrael ote hee l'olam,
Kee shayshet yameem asah Adonai
Et ha-shamahyeem v'et ha-aretz
Oo-vah yome ha-shveeyee Shavaht vah-eenahfahsh.

The Israelites are to observe the Sabbath,
Celebrating it for the generations to come
    as an everlasting covenant.
It will be a sign between me and the Israelites forever,
For in six days the Lord made the heavens and the earth,
And on the seventh day he abstained from work and rested.

2. LIGHTING OF THE CANDLES

■ Mother says:

As I light our Shabbat candles to set apart this special gift for our family, may all of us be reminded that it is the light of Messiah that shines in us and in our home. As I cover my eyes may we be reminded that before Messiah opens our eyes of understanding, we cannot see the glories and the joy of all that his light sheds understanding on. I spread the light of the candles with my hands throughout our home to express my desire as wife and mother that the light of Messiah and the joy of his Sabbath rest be spread throughout our home.

At this time, the "Sabbath Song" (in Appendix B) or some other song may be sung.

The mother now lights the candles and covers her eyes with both hands. The lighting of the candles is traditionally reserved for women. We suggest that it affords an opportunity for the mother to teach her daughters about the place of women in the home by way of example. On occasion she may even let a daughter light the candles and say the blessings.

■ She prays:

בָּרוּךְ אַתָּה, יְיָ אֱלֹהֵינוּ, מֶלֶךְ הָעוֹלָם,
אֲשֶׁר קִדְּשָׁנוּ בְּמִצְוֹתָיו וְצִוָּנוּ לְהַדְלִיק נֵר שֶׁל שַׁבָּת.

Barukh atah Adonai Elohenu melekh ha-olam, asher kidshanu b'mitzvohtav v'tzi-vanu l'hadleek ner shel Shabbat.

Blessed art thou, O Lord our God, King of the universe, who has set us apart by your commandments and has commanded us to kindle the Sabbath lights.

The Bible does not directly command us to "kindle the Sabbath lights." However, to a Jewish mind, kindling the Sabbath lights is a symbolic gesture to set Shabbat apart, which the Bible does command.

19

■ Here is an appropriate alternate blessing:

בָּרוּךְ אַתָּה, יְיָ אֱלֹהֵינוּ, מֶלֶךְ הָעוֹלָם,
אֲשֶׁר קִדְּשָׁנוּ בְּמִצְוֹתָיו וְצִוָּנוּ לִהְיוֹת אוֹר
לְגוֹיִים וְנָתַן-לָנוּ יֵשׁוּעַ מְשִׁיחֵנוּ הָאוֹר לָעוֹלָם.

*Barukh atah Adonai Elohenu melekh ha-olam, asher kidshanu
b'mitzvohtav l'hayot or l'goyeem v'natan-lanu Yeshua
m'sheekhaynu ha-or la-olam.*

*Blessed art thou, O Lord our God, King of the universe, who has
sanctified us by thy commandments and commanded us to be a
light unto the nations and has given us Yeshua, our Messiah, the
Light of the World.*

3. THE HAND-WASHING

The mother brings out a bowl and pitcher for handwashing.

■ Read:

*The earth is the LORD's, and everything in it, the world, and all who
live in it; for he founded it upon the seas and established it upon
the waters. Who may ascend the hill of the LORD? Who may stand
in his holy place? He who has clean hands and a pure heart, who
does not lift up his soul to an idol or swear by what is false* (Psalm
24:1–4).

■ All in turn, as they wash their hands, say:

I dedicate my hands to Messiah, the hope of glory, to serve him only.

4. BLESSING OVER WINE

■ The father pours wine or grape juice into the goblets, saying:

*In Jewish thought the wine represents joy. When we lift the cup of
wine and recite the suggested blessing, called the* Kiddush, *we are*

really thanking God for all the joy that he gives us. Since we are believers in Yeshua, we indeed have much for which we should bless God. In the context of this Erev Shabbat time, we are especially thanking the Lord for giving us the Shabbat and for giving us the eternal rest we have in Messiah. So, by raising this cup of joy, we are expressing to each other and to the Lord, the joy that we have by faith in Messiah.

בָּרוּךְ אַתָּה, יְיָ אֱלֹהֵינוּ, מֶלֶךְ הָעוֹלָם, בּוֹרֵא פְּרִי הַגָּפֶן.

Barukh atah Adonai Elohenu melekh ha-olam, boray p'ree ha-gahfen.

Blessed art thou, O Lord our God, King of the universe, who creates the fruit of the vine.

All at the table take a sip of wine or grape juice.

5. THE CHALLAH

■ Read:

As a blanket of dew covered the double portion of manna in the wilderness every sixth day, so the challah is covered. Why do we celebrate Shabbat with two challot? Because as our people wandered in the desert, the Lord our God provided all of our needs. He is the Lord who provides. He never asks us to do something we are unable to do. During our wanderings in the desert, he provided a double portion of manna on the sixth day so that we would not need to go out to gather on the seventh. Also, the challah is a symbol of Yeshua, the Bread of Life who is our Life.

The readings for the wine and bread could be done by asking the children for the information rather than the father merely reciting it. This method is the popular version in our house. It serves as an additional teaching tool for the children. There are four children in the Berkowitz family, and each week we ask one to carefully remove the challah cover and fold it. This custom involves the children in the order of service. They all look forward to this honor.

■ Father passes a piece of challah to each person, and leads in *Hamotzi:*

בָּרוּךְ אַתָּה, יְיָ אֱלֹהֵינוּ, מֶלֶךְ הָעוֹלָם,
הַמּוֹצִיא לֶחֶם מִן הָאָרֶץ.

*Barukh atah Adonai Elohenu melekh ha-olam, ha-motzee lekhem
meen ha-aretz.*

*Blessed art Thou, O Lord our God, King of the universe, who
brings forth bread from the earth.*

6. BLESSING FOR THE MOTHER

■ Father now recites *Aishet Khayeel*, The Virtuous Woman, Proverbs
31:10–31. The husband reads this passage in order to bless and honor
his wife.

7. BLESSING THE CHILDREN

■ Father and mother, placing their hands on each child's head,
pronounce the blessing found in Torah:

יְבָרֶכְךָ יְיָ וְיִשְׁמְרֶךָ.
יָאֵר יְיָ פָּנָיו אֵלֶיךָ וִיחֻנֶּךָ.
יִשָּׂא יְיָ פָּנָיו אֵלֶיךָ, וְיָשֵׂם לְךָ שָׁלוֹם.

Y'varekh'khah Adonai v'yishm'rekhah.
Ya'er Adonai panav elekhah vee-khunekhah.
Yeesah Adonai panav elekhah, v'yahsaym l'khah shalom.

The Lord bless you and keep you.
The Lord make his face to shine upon you and be gracious unto you.
The Lord lift up his face upon you and give you peace.

■ Blessing your sons, say:

יְשִׂמְךָ אֱלֹהִים כְּאֶפְרַיִם וְכִמְנַשֶּׁה.

Y'simkhah Elohim k'Ephrayeem v'kheeM'nasheh.

May God make you like Ephraim and Manasseh.

■ Blessing your daughters, say:

יְשִׂמֵךְ אֱלֹהִים כְּשָׂרָה, רִבְקָה, רָחֵל וְלֵאָה.

Y'simekh Elohim k'Sarah, Rivkah, Rakhel, v'Leah.

May God make you like Sarah, Rebekah, Rachel and Leah.

■ You may also want to use the well-known Sabbath prayer, popularized in *Fiddler on the Roof,* to teach your family and add further beauty to your time together.

■ All greet each other:

Shabbat shalom, Shabbat shalom, Shabbat shalom.
May the peace of God be with you always.
Shabbat shalom.
(See Appendix B for Shabbat music.)

8. THE MEAL

The meal follows with leisurely family fellowship as its main course! The food tastes special on the Sabbath because Sabbath itself forms one of its ingredients! An anecdote from the Talmud illustrates this:

Once, Rabbi Judah, the Prince, invited the Emperor to a Sabbath meal. "This food tastes like no other I have ever eaten," the emperor exclaimed. "Give me your recipe!" "I cannot do so," the rabbi replied. "We have a special spice; it is called the Sabbath *and it gives its special taste to every morsel consumed in Jewish homes on the holy day"* (Sabbath 119a).

We find it to be true!

9. AFTER THE MEAL

The time following the meal could be spent singing some family songs together. See Appendix B for suggestions. In addition, if you have *Erev Shabbat* services, you're all dressed and ready to go! If not, enjoy the special blessings of an early bed time.

We would also like to suggest the following. If you do not have *Erev Shabbat* services, this Friday evening meal is an excellent time to invite guests into your home. Perhaps you could invite another person or family from your congregation. You might also use this time to invite someone who does not know Messiah. Conducting a Friday evening meal in such a fashion as we have described is conducive to making a Jewish family feel at home and is a good discussion stimulator!

SHABBAT MORNING

In planning your day together as a family, keep in mind the discussion of Sabbath and its purpose. The plans you make for the Sabbath day should facilitate the family members relating to each other as Messiah would relate to each of us. Any plans that would detract from maintaining this attitude would defeat the purpose of Shabbat. Remember, the day was given as a gift—its purpose being to have an entire day set aside *without distraction.* Thus, we can practice keeping our mind and body yielded to Messiah in all that we do and say. Be creative as a family in your plans. You could have a special family planning session during the week and take advantage of your children's wonderful ideas.

Here are some suggestions to get you started:
■ sleep late (if you can)
■ play games (Bible Trivia, The Ungame)
■ Saturday afternoon looking at home movies, slides, family albums

- let the children reminisce with you about the pictures; discuss how God is helping them to grow up
- take a walk in your neighborhood
- fellowship with someone in your congregation
- go for a hike
- go on a picnic
- play music together
- walk on the beach or discover nature
- read, read, read!
- nap
- visit a nursing or old folks home
- do a *secret drop* for someone you know who has a material need. Go to their house, and let one child sneak up to their door and leave the package. Then scamper away secretly and quickly!

What you eat on Shabbat may vary. The important thing to keep in mind is to make as little fuss and work as possible. At this time, all the preparation for Shabbat done during the week will come in handy. Perhaps you can just bring out a pre-prepared dish. Perhaps you can have some already-made sandwiches in the refrigerator. You may also just want to eat the leftovers from Friday night.

Jewish tradition prescribes three meals on Shabbat:
- Erev Shabbat (Friday evening)
- Shabbat, approximately noon on Saturday
- Shabbat evening

Could this suggest sleeping late Saturday morning, going to services and then having a brunch when you get home? Sounds good to us! How about you?

It is also important to note that Yeshua healed on the Sabbath. He was criticized for it, but he taught through his acts that he is Lord of the Sabbath, thereby making his activities those which should govern our day. Hence, if the Lord leads you to help someone on Shabbat, do it! It is a day when the needs of the total person are met by the Lord. God may want to use you to meet someone's needs.

HAVDALAH

Shabbat comes to an end after the evening meal. Some don't close Shabbat until well after sundown, when evening *officially* begins (traditionally when three stars are visible). In whatever way the ending of Shabbat is determined, if this day is properly spent, it is usually a sad occasion. It is like saying farewell to your best friend!

Because of this feeling, many Jewish people conduct what is called *Havdalah*. This service is brief yet full of beautiful symbolism. We find these traditions meaningful to our family life. We hope you will, too. In fact, as you will see, we have even made up some new traditions of our own which are helpful to us as Messianic Jews. You may want to do the same.

Havdalah means *separation*. Havdalah is a time when the family formally bids farewell to the Shabbat by reinforcing its distinction from the rest of the days of the week. These helpful traditions serve to enhance our family life and facilitate further connectedness with our fellow Jews. With the proper attitude, Havdalah will help create in us the distinctiveness of Shabbat and increase our appreciation for this gift which God has given our people.

The evening has arrived. The table is cleared. To celebrate Havdalah you will need the following traditional *and* non-traditional items, many of which can be purchased in a Jewish bookstore. Keep in mind, this is the way we Berkowitz*im* celebrate Havdalah and is offered *only* as a pattern or suggestion. We hope you will find your own way of doing it better!

■ wine or grape juice
■ Kiddush cup and saucer
■ a Havdalah candle, or two plain candles
■ spice box

■ sweet spices
■ a small plate with a small vase
■ a piece of left-over challah on a special plate
■ a Bible
■ a Siddur (prayer book)

The special plate and small vase are used in an observance we have devised. The vase is to be full of water or salt-water and placed in the middle of the plate.

For a special remembrance, we place the piece of challah on a plate with birds painted on it. You may want to buy a special one from a nicknack shop. The easiest way to obtain a special plate would be to have your children draw or cut out pictures of birds to decorate a plain plate. The reason for the birds will become evident soon.

1. LIGHT THE HAVDALAH CANDLE

Havdalah begins with the lighting of the special candle. If no Havdalah candle is available, two ordinary candles can be lit with the flames joining at the top in an upsidedown V. No blessing is said yet. Lighting the candles at the outset, after sundown, when considered with the candle lighting at the start of Shabbat, sets apart (sanctifies) this day.

2. READING FROM SCRIPTURE

■ Read Psalm 128, and read or sing Isaiah 12:2–3 (traditional).

3. DRINK FROM THE KIDDUSH CUP

Next, the father fills the Kiddush cup with wine or grape juice so that it overflows into a saucer. We usually follow the order found in the Ashkenazi Siddur because we are from an Ashkenazi background. We are not familiar with the Sephardic service.

■ Explain the overflowing Kiddush Cup.

The joy that Shabbat gives us is overflowing. We are able to be a family, to worship the Lord, to rest, and to be reminded again of the Shabbat-rest we possess by faith in Yeshua. May this joy carry us through the week.

Note that we made Shabbat special with a Kiddush (a sanctification or setting apart) at its beginning, and we close it with another Kiddush at its end.

■ Recite the blessing over the wine and partake.

בָּרוּךְ אַתָּה, יְיָ אֱלֹהֵינוּ, מֶלֶךְ הָעוֹלָם, בּוֹרֵא פְּרִי הַגָּפֶן.

Barukh atah Adonai Elohenu melekh ha-olam, boray p'ree ha-gahfen.

Blessed art thou, O Lord our God, King of the universe, who creates the fruit of the vine.

4. SMELL THE SWEET SPICES

■ Explain the spices:

May the remembrance of the Shabbat be as sweet to us as these sweet spices are.

■ Recite the blessing for the spices.

בָּרוּךְ אַתָּה, יְיָ אֱלֹהֵינוּ, מֶלֶךְ הָעוֹלָם, בּוֹרֵא מִינֵי בְשָׂמִים.

Barukh atah Adonai Elohenu melekh ha-olam, boray meenay b'sameem.

Blessed are you, O Lord our God, King of the universe, who creates the fragrant spices.

Pass the spice box around for all to get a good smell of the sweet aroma. Be sure to take a big whiff! Symbolically, we try to keep the sweetness of Shabbat with us as long as we can.

5. DISCUSS THE HAVDALAH CANDLE

■ Turning your attention back to the lit candle, explain the multi-wick.

Shabbat has brightened our life as we get both physical and spiritual rest. Our eyes again have been focused on Yeshua, our Shabbat, the light of the world. Lighting the candle as the first act of the new week reminds us too, that God's first act of creation took place when he said, "Let there be light." We now bid Shabbat farewell by lighting the Havdalah candle, giving even more light than when Shabbat began.

■ Recite the blessing for the candle.
(You may let one of the children hold the candle.)

בָּרוּךְ אַתָּה, יְיָ אֱלֹהֵינוּ, מֶלֶךְ הָעוֹלָם,
בּוֹרֵא מְאוֹרֵי הָאֵשׁ.

Barukh atah Adonai Elohenu melekh ha-olam, boray m'oray ha-aysh.

Blessed are you, O Lord our God, King of the universe, who creates the light of the fire.

6. RECITE THE HAVDALAH BLESSING

בָּרוּךְ אַתָּה, יְיָ אֱלֹהֵינוּ, מֶלֶךְ הָעוֹלָם,
הַמַּבְדִּיל בֵּין קֹדֶשׁ לְחֹל, בֵּין אוֹר לְחֹשֶׁךְ,
בֵּין יִשְׂרָאֵל לָעַמִּים,
בֵּין יוֹם הַשְׁבִיעִי לְשֵׁשֶׁת יְמֵי הַמַּעֲשֶׂה.
בָּרוּךְ אַתָּה, יְיָ, הַמַּבְדִּיל בֵּין קֹדֶשׁ לְחֹל.

Barukh atah Adonai Elohenu melekh ha-olam,
Ha-mavdeel bayn kodesh l'khol, bayn or l'khoshekh,
Bayn Yisrael l'ameem,
Bayn yom ha-shveeyee le-shayshet y'may ha-ma'aseh.

Barukh atah Adonai, ha-mavdeel bayn kodesh l'khol.

Blessed are you, Lord our God, King of the universe who makes a division between the sacred and the secular, between light and darkness, between Israel and the other nations, between the seventh day and the six working days. Blessed are you, Lord, who makes a distinction between the secular and the sacred.

It is customary to read and/or sing Isaiah 12, "Behold, God is my salvation."

7. EXTINGUISH THE CANDLE IN THE WINE

■ The traditional Jewish symbolism is unclear at this point. However, may we suggest the following:

May the light and joy of Shabbat be mixed together into one, reflecting the truth that Yeshua is the one true source for both. May this statement stay with us this coming week.

8. PASS THE WATER VASE (A Berkowitz Tradition)

■ Father read Luke 7:36–38.

In Biblical times it was a custom of our people to keep a specially shaped vase called a "tear cup." It was shaped to fit against one's cheek under the eye. In times of sadness or grief, tears were stored by letting them fall into this cup. Miriam (Luke 7:37 and John 11:2) had found the Messiah, and, sitting at his feet, he filled her every need. She no longer had any need of her tear cup for the storing up of her many tears. She poured both her tears and conceivably her tear cup on the feet of the Messiah and gazed up into his face, her cup of joy filled and overflowing.

As the family sings, *I Love You Lord,* or some similar song, the small vase of water and a bowl are passed around. Everyone pours a little water into the bowl. This symbolically shows us pouring out our tears to Yeshua, implying, "This week I will choose to submit my feelings to the Lord and let him do his work in my life. For, just as Miriam trusted her sorrows, griefs, trials, and heartbreak to Yeshua, so we will choose to do the same this coming week."

9. EAT CHALLAH (Another Berkowitz Custom)

■ Reading of Matthew 6:25–34 by one of the children.

The father or mother explains that just as God takes care of birds and flowers and provides for them, even more so will he take care of us. Are we not worth more to him? We are told not to worry because he will treat us as his special creation. As this is being explained, the special plate—decorated with birds to keep with the motif of Matthew 6:25–34—with a slice of leftover challah from Friday evening's meal is passed around. Everyone takes a small piece, and then we pray. As we pray, we look forward to the next week. In faith, we tell the Lord that we will choose to set our minds on him, trusting that he will provide all we need according to his grace and wisdom, just as he did this past week (symbolized by the leftover challah).

10. CONCLUDE HAVDALAH

Havdalah is now complete. A common greeting would be, *Shavuah Tov*, which means, "Have a good week!" Traditionally, a light desert is enjoyed at this point.

PART III

A CHALLENGE TO MESSIANIC JEWS AND GENTILES!

We have studied some key biblical teaching regarding the Sabbath. We have shown that Shabbat is a visible symbol of God's covenant with Israel as a *called-out* nation. We have seen the ways in which Shabbat serves as a weekly picture to the family of what it is like to be properly related to God by resting in the finished work of Messiah Yeshua. We have shared how Shabbat observance can enhance our spiritual lives and the joy God wants us to experience.

In the second section, we presented you with some practical ways to observe Shabbat to honor the Lord's intended purpose for it. All the while, we have consistently reminded you that as Messianic Jews and Gentiles, we do not observe Shabbat hoping to earn, merit, keep or add to the wonderful gift of salvation which the Lord has given us by faith in Messiah.

By now, your bagel is just a memory and that easy chair you reclined in to read this book has relaxed every part of you. But *wait*! You haven't finished!

In order to appreciate and understand fully what we've been saying, please read the book of *Nehemiah*. We'll wait! Don't get side-tracked by the details; just read it through in one sitting to see the message God has for us and our people. Here is what God wants us to consider.

We *must* rebuild! God has been rebuilding Israel for several decades in both a physical and spiritual sense. Someday, those of us in the *diaspora* may realize the full significance of Nehemiah's message by rebuilding Jerusalem physically. But for now, let us apply the rebuilding message of Nehemiah spiritually.

To do so, first think of the spiritual rebuilding necessary in our own personal lives, then in our families, and then among the Jewish nation as a whole. When we do that, we will quickly see—as did Nehemiah—that the protective walls God intends for us to have are in disrepair. We are talking here of Scripture, especially the Torah. As a people, we have simply let this wall lie in shambles.

Because of its condition, the enemies of God—worldliness, disobedience, disrespect, mistrust, unholiness and darkness—have had a detrimental impact upon us and our people. God wants us to begin to mend that wall of protection now as a remnant people. When we do so his glory will shine in the temples of our lives. But, it all starts with Shabbat.

If we take God's teachings regarding Shabbat seriously it will help mend the rest of the broken wall. Then we will know and experience the *real* rest, protection, and fruitfulness God intends for us and our people, Israel. To be more specific, meditate on the following comparisons.

Just as Nehemiah saw the deplorable condition of Jerusalem, so may the Lord give us spiritual eyes to see the weakened condition of Israel. Just as Nehemiah admonished the small company of Israelites to *come rebuild the walls and gates which lie in ruins*, so too does God call us. He has raised up a unity of Messianic Jews who spiritually dwell in the land of promise. May we now, in unity, respond as did our forefathers. *Let us start rebuilding now!*

The Israelites had enemies around them. So do we! There are those who do not understand, who ridicule and mock. But let us answer as did the Israelites: *the joy of the Lord is our strength.*

Finally, just as the Israelites rebuilt the walls in front of their houses, may we, too, begin to rebuild the beauty of living God's Law as Messianic people. God's glory will once again shine forth from our midst. We will indeed be lights to the nations, and our homes will be like rebuilt *golden gates* enabling many to enter into their rest in Messiah.

If you can see the importance of all of this then begin by observing Shabbat in God's way and for God's reasons. How about this week? When you do, after the dishes are cleared and the children are in bed, take time to enjoy the soft light of the flickering flames of the candles you lit. In this mellow moment, try to imagine your forefathers listening to Moses as he instructed them in the wilderness. Let your thoughts go through the centuries following, feeling for your people. Let the candles enlighten you so you can see Nehemiah leading his people to rebuild the walls and Ezra the priest reading the Law.

Finally, may you see Messiah, the light of the world. He wants to speak to you in the quietness of this Shabbat through his word by means of his spirit. He wants you to pray for your people and those whom God has chosen, that they too may find real *rest* in him.

In light of God's word, may you now begin and continue to bless the Lord our God by making his Shabbat a delight to your soul.

APPENDIX A

SATURDAY OR SUNDAY?

We have emphasized the importance of observing Shabbat the way God intended, focusing on the seventh day. If you are a non-Jewish believer, you might be wondering, "This is fine for Messianic *Jews*. For you the Sabbath certainly is Saturday. But what about me? Isn't the Christian's Sabbath Sunday?"

This is a tough question and needs careful consideration. We don't want to tell anyone what to do. But perhaps if we present a little background with which you may be unfamiliar, it will help clarify your thinking. However, we should say here that worship on *any* day of the week, or better yet, on *every* day of the week is fine with us. It's just that the Shabbat has special spiritual significance.

First, let us state unequivocally, God did not change the Sabbath from Saturday to Sunday. "How is it then," you might ask, "that most Christians worship on Sunday?" This is a good question.

Some conclude from certain New Covenant verses that God indeed did change the day of rest. Revelation 1:10 is often quoted to indicate that a new day of worship has come. The NIV, KJV, NASB all use the words commonly used by Christians to refer to Sunday, "the Lord's Day." This describes *when* John was "in the Spirit." The thinking then is that a *new* day of worship was affirmed by John. However, there are other ways to understand these words.

The JNT, for example, translates them, "the day of the Lord." This term has prophetic significance and may be more accurate. Some see this expression as a description of the kind of day it was—a lordly day. Sort of an adjective. Further, who is to say that John was not referring to the seventh-day Sabbath?

In whatever way it is translated, it does not indicate a change in the day of worship, nor for that matter, does it speak of the day being Sunday, Saturday or any other Sabbath day. Chances are it is not discussing any particular day of the week.

The second idea that *seems* to indicate that the day of worship changed is the fact that the believers met on the first day of the week. It is true that they did. However, in Israel then, and to this day, the first day of the week begins on Saturday evening.

A good example of this is found in Acts 20:7–12. Here it is stated that the believers met "on the first day of the week," broke bread, and had a meeting where Paul preached. The Jewish custom was to meet for a third Sabbath meal just before the Sabbath is over. The meal is called *Saidah Shlishi*, or *Shalosh Seudot*. This could have been the breaking of bread mentioned in verse 7. Traditionally, after this meal and the close of Shabbat, Havdalah begins.

The passage itself indicates that they were meeting at night. Paul preached until midnight which would have made an awfully long talk if he had begun on Sunday morning, the "first" day of the week. Further, in Israel the first day of the week is a work-day, mitigating against a Sunday service. And if the Sabbath had been changed to Sunday, Paul would not have traveled on that day as he did. Traveling on the Sabbath was forbidden, and Paul was zealous for the Law.

It becomes clear that the biblical passages often cited to show a change in the Sabbath day, or at least the day of worship, don't support this conclusion.

Most theologians will tell you to base your understanding of the Bible on the word of God, itself, not historical practice. This is particularly true for the day of the week on which to observe God's Sabbath. The biblical texts teach the seventh-day Sabbath. How then did the Sabbath come to be observed on the first day of the week?

Dr. Samuele Bacchiocchi, in an article he wrote for the *Biblical Archaelogy Review* (Sept./Oct., 1978, pp. 32–29) cited Acts 15; 21:21 and some early church fathers (Eusebius and Epiphanius) to stress that "both the ethnic composition and the theological orientation of the Jerusalem Church were profoundly Jewish....It would be unthinkable that this Church at this early time would change the Sabbath to Sunday." In fact he states that the Nazarenes (Messianic Jews) kept a Saturday Shabbat until well into the fourth century. He stated clearly that "Sabbath keeping was one of this church's distinguishing characteristics."

When, then, did the change to Sunday take place and for what reason?

Bacchiocchi is emphatic when he suggests that the evidence points to sometime after 135 C.E. The reason? Anti-semitism!

The history is clear. After the second Jewish revolt in 135 C.E., the emperor Hadrian began to issue strict anti-Jewish legislation. The Babylonian Talmud comments on some of the legislation:

> *The government of Rome issued a decree that they [the Jews] should not study Torah, and that they should not circumcise their sons, and that they should profane the Sabbath* (Rosh Hashana 19a).

In order to show that it was not Jewish, and, therefore, not subject to the persecution directed against the Jews after 135 C.E., "the Church of Rome adopted concerted measures to wean the Christians away from the Sabbath veneration in order to enhance Sunday worship exclusively." In fact, eventually a Saturday fast was introduced.

Commenting on this, Sylvester (314–333 C.E.) said that it was intended to "show contempt for the Jews" and to "avoid appearing to observe the Sabbath with the Jews." Finally, Bacchiocchi says that it was not until the Council of Nicea in the mid-fourth century that the idea of connecting the Sunday Sabbath with the Resurrection Day began to be universally propagated (although it had been introduced many years before this).

Bacchiocchi concludes, therefore, saying, "It seems clear that the Sunday observance originated in Rome in the early part of the second century (but after 135)." He states that it was not for biblical reasons that the Sabbath was changed, but for expediency for the gentile church to avoid any Jewish connection and avoid persecution of them by an anti-Jewish Roman government.

Given all this, what should a gentile believer do here in the twentieth century? In our opinion, three conclusions suggest themselves.

First, the Church should accept and encourage seventh-day Sabbath keeping by Messianic Jews. The Scriptures support this practice as we've shown. Shabbat did not change during Bible times. And there is especially good reason to observe the seventh day.

The creation God made is perfect and beautiful. Each intricate detail was designed by the Master Designer for a purpose just as it is. The biblical holiday cycle (Leviticus 23) is part of this creation. It is like a jeweled watch, each holiday on the face of the dial represented by a beautiful gemstone. To move the jewels around does a disservice to the watchmaker, the creator.

Shabbat is like a jewel in the cycle of revelation. God established this cycle and said these days are to be observed *at their appointed times*. No other holidays have been tampered with. Only Shabbat. Does man have the right to tamper with the beautiful work of the Creator? If he placed the jewel of Shabbat on the seventh day, how can man change that day.

Second, the Church needs to understand and admit that the Bible neither teaches nor requires changing the Sabbath from the seventh day to the first. Sunday, like any other day, is a fine day to worship. But it is not the Lord's Shabbat.

Last, while Acts 15 makes it clear that the gentile believers are not required to observe Shabbat, the Church would do well to study the issue more closely. Since believers are free to observe if they chose, they might receive an extra blessing if they do.

Exodus 20:10 hints at this idea stating that the "stranger" living among Israel should keep Shabbat. Who is the "stranger" living among Israel. Our answer—the gentile believer who has been "grafted-in" (Romans 11:16-24) and become part of the "commonwealth of Israel" (Ephesians 2:12 NASB).

So we say be careful how you interpret the Bible particularly concerning the Sabbath. God put it where he put it for good reason. Rather, consider enjoying this special day of blessing, given to all God's people as a sign of his commitment to us and a picture of the Sabbath-rest the believer has in Messiah.

APPENDIX B

SHABBAT RECIPES

Even though we are including some recipes, we have also decided to tell you how to find your own. Here are the best resources.

If you have a Jewish grandmother, she is the best resource for anything Jewish! What she can't remember, your mother and aunts will! Besides, what a great way to keep the relationships going! Why not invite them over for an *Erev Shabbat* meal?

If you don't have a Jewish grandmother, the following books will be helpful.

Jewish Cookery by Leah W. Leonard, Crown Publishers, NY, 1949.

Guide for the Jewish Homemaker by Shonie B. Levi and Sylvia R. Kaplan, Schocken books, NY, 1959.

The Children's Jewish Holiday Kitchen by Joan Nathan, Schocken Books, NY, 1987.

And there are many more.

Let us take this opportunity to share some of *our* favorite recipes for a delicious *Erev Shabbat* dinner.

HOME MADE CHALLAH
From the Berkowitz kitchen!

INGREDIENTS:
8 cups of white unbleached flour
1/2 cup of honey
4 Tbls. melted butter
2 cups warm potato water or plain water
2 Tbls. yeast
3 slightly beaten eggs

If whole grain challah is desired, substitute white flour with
2 cups whole wheat flour
2 cups barley flour
4 cups unbleached white flour

INSTRUCTIONS:
1. Place flour in a large bowl.
2. Mix honey, melted butter, and water. Set aside 1 cup of the liquid.
3. Dissolve yeast in 1 cup of the liquid; when bubbly—make a well in the flour and pour the liquid in.
4. Add 3 slightly beaten eggs. Add the remaining liquid and stir. Stir in the remaining flour from the sides of the bowl; form a dough ball.
5. Turn out the dough and knead thoroughly while praying for the children (see page 16).
6. Place dough in a bowl, cover and let rise until double in bulk.
7. Knead again, and divide into sections for 2 large loaves and 1 *baby* loaf.
8. Between lightly floured hands, roll dough into 3 strips of even length. Braid them togther. Repeat for the second loaf and *baby* loaf. Two large loaves will fit on 1 oiled cookie sheet.
9. Bake loaves at 375° for 30 minutes.

HOME MADE CHALLAH COVER

Instructions for a challah cover follow. This is a cross-stitch anyone in the family could make.

From *Celebrate the Feasts* by Martha Zimmerman. This book is available through LEDERER PUBLICATIONS. Used by permission.

ONE POT CHICKEN

INGREDIENTS:

5 pound chicken
2 large onions
fresh garlic
tumeric
6 Tbls. ketchup
2 Tbls. worcestershire sauce

4–5 large potatoes
2 large carrots
paprika
2 Tbls. soy sauce
1 cup water

INSTRUCTIONS:

1. Thoroughly clean chicken and place in large roasting pan.

2. Cut up potatoes, carrots and onions and place around the chicken. Put a few onions on top of the chicken.

3. Sprinkle fresh garlic, tumeric, paprika all over chicken.

4. Pour ketchup, soy sauce, worcestershire sauce, and water over all. Cover roasting pan.

5. Place in oven at 375° for 2½–3 hours. Test chicken for tenderness. The leg should be loose enough to nearly separate from the chicken just by pulling.

6. Remove and slice chicken. It's nice to separate the dark and light meat. Place in a deep baking dish. Cover chicken with onions and juice from roasting pan. Cover dish. Place in oven at 300°.

7. In a separate baking dish, place potatoes, carrots and onions with some of the juice and cover.

8. Keep both dishes in the oven at 300° until ready to serve dinner.

BRISKET

INGREDIENTS:

5 lbs. beef brisket	2 large onions
1 pkg Lipton onion soup mix	paprika
garlic	water

INSTRUCTIONS:

1. Slice or dice two large onions. Place on bottom of a very large soup pot.

2. Place beef brisket on top of onions.

3. Pour onion soup mix over the beef and onions

4. Liberally sprinkle garlic powder and a little paprika over all the ingredients.

5. Pour approximately one-half cup of water over all.

Cover pot and cook on top of stove on a low fire for a minimum of three hours, turning beef over periodically. Cook until beef is very tender but not falling apart, otherwise it will be stringy. Cut fat off top of brisket and slice beef across grain. Put slices into an oven-proof baking dish and pour juices and onions on top; cover and place in oven at 300°. This will serve four people.

SONGS FOR SHABBAT

You can obtain songs for Shabbat at most Jewish bookstores or by contacting LEDERER PUBLICATIONS for a beautiful cassette of Shabbat songs and other Messianic music. A sample of a Messianic Shabbat song follows.

SHABBAT SONG
by Devorah Goldberg

BIBLIOGRAPHY

Bacchiocci, Dr. Samuel. "How it Came About: From Saturday to Sunday." *Biblical Archaeology Review*, September/October 1978, 32–39.

Driver, Brown, and Briggs, eds. *A Hebrew and English Lexicon of the Old Testament*. Oxford: The Clarendon Press, 1907.

Frost, Siegmund. *Shabbat Shalom*. New York: General Israel Orphan's Home for Girls, 1978.

Juster, Daniel C. *Jewish Roots*. Rockville, Md: Davar, 1986.

Kolatch, Alfred J. *The Jewish Book of Why*. Middle Village, NY: Jonathan David Publishers, 1981.

Leonard, Leah W. *Jewish Cookery*. New York: Crown Publishers, 1949.

Levi, Shonie B., and Sylvia R. Kaplan. *Guide for the Jewish Homemaker*. NY: Schocken Books, 1978.

Needham, David C. *Birthright*. Portland: Multnomah Press, 1979.

Nichol, Richard C. Resolved: Jewish Believers Are Obligated to Observe Shabbat. Typescript.

Saypol, Judyth R., and Madeline Wikler. *Come, Let Us Welcome Shabbat*. Rockville, Md: Kar-Ben Copies, 1978.

Scherman, Rabbi Nosson. *The Complete Art Schroll Siddur (Ashkenaz)*. Brooklyn: Mesorah Publishers, 1986.

Trepp, Rabbi Leo. *The Complete Book of Jewish Observance*. New York: Behrman House, Summit Books, 1980.

Other materials distributed by LEDERER to help you enjoy a worshipful SHABBAT:

Shabbat candle holders
Challah covers
Havdalah sets
Kiddush cups
Men's and women's head coverings
Men's prayer shawls

Children's curriculum for the Sabbath

Delight in the Sabbath
music cassette by Jonathan Settel

God's Appointed Times
by Barney Kasdan
Celebrate the Feasts
by Martha Zimmerman
two books that will help you fully appreciate Shabbat
and the other Biblical celebrations

These are just some of the books and products
that Lederer publishes or distributes.
For a FREE catalog featuring Messianic literature,
Scripture, Messianic music CD's and cassettes,
as well as Judaica gift items,
write or call:

LEDERER

6204 Park Heights Avenue
Baltimore, MD 21215
(410) 358-6471